THE
STUDY OF ECONOMIC HISTORY

T0346176

THE
STUDY OF ECONOMIC HISTORY
An Inaugural Lecture

BY

J. H. CLAPHAM, Litt.D., F.B.A.

Professor of Economic History
and Fellow of King's
College

CAMBRIDGE
AT THE UNIVERSITY PRESS
1929

CAMBRIDGE
UNIVERSITY PRESS

University Printing House, Cambridge CB2 8BS, United Kingdom

Published in the United States of America by Cambridge University Press, New York

Cambridge University Press is part of the University of Cambridge.

It furthers the University's mission by disseminating knowledge in the pursuit of education, learning and research at the highest international levels of excellence.

www.cambridge.org
Information on this title: www.cambridge.org/9781107674264

© Cambridge University Press 1929

This publication is in copyright. Subject to statutory exception and to the provisions of relevant collective licensing agreements, no reproduction of any part may take place without the written permission of Cambridge University Press.

First published 1929
Re-issued 2014

A catalogue record for this publication is available from the British Library

ISBN 978-1-107-67426-4 Paperback

Cambridge University Press has no responsibility for the persistence or accuracy of URLs for external or third-party internet websites referred to in this publication, and does not guarantee that any content on such websites is, or will remain, accurate or appropriate.

The
STUDY OF ECONOMIC HISTORY

THIS chair of economic history which Cambridge has set up, and to which she has done me the honour of calling me, is— by an odd accident—at this moment the only chair of economic history in the Kingdom. There have been two others—the first, very appropriately, at Manchester, left vacant of late by the premature death of the keenest economic historian and one of the most single-minded scholars of my generation, George Unwin; and the second in London, also vacated by untimely death, the death of a Cambridge historian, Lilian Knowles, who spent her working life in building up the historical side of the London School of Economics. For the time being, but for reasons not connected with the academic valuation of economic history, these Universities—like Oxford and many others—are

5

carrying on with readerships. There are happily besides the readers scholars of professorial quality, though I fear seldom with professorial leisure, working at the subject unlabelled or otherwise labelled—historians with economic interests, economists with historical leanings, professors of commerce, readers in currency. Lecturers in economic history are numerous; for every year, from the elementary schools up to the universities, there is a call for teachers—teachers of economic history pure; of social history which requires an economic substratum; of local history which requires one also; and of the widening study of "human geography," as the French say, which can no more dispense with economic history than economic history can dispense with it. If university chairs are, in wilfully mixed metaphor, the crown and fountain-head of what they call in Germany a *Disciplin*—an organized body of studies—it will, I think, be agreed that this Discipline of Economic History is lightly crowned and in some present danger of being but lightly refreshed. For the future I have no fear. The

6

thing is growing and will grow. There are whole tracts still to be occupied. Three specialist journals in English have been started in the last three years, and new syntheses should be coming soon. My single regret, when I think of its relatively late recognition in this University, is that the man who nursed it here, and who was known in all Universities as one of the two outstanding English economic historians of his time, William Cunningham, never received from Cambridge the professorial rank which he deserved. Nor, for that matter, did his rather younger colleague, Sir William Ashley, from Oxford.

As a borderline study, lying along the frontiers of history and economics, with an ill-defined territory over which both the general historians and the economists require —so to speak—grazing rights, its late acquisition of academic independence is natural. Political economy as an established university study is itself young and history not so very old. True, Adam Smith was a professor; but, like Henry Sidgwick here, he professed moral philosophy. He was a pensioner of the Duke of Buccleuch when he wrote the *Wealth of Nations*; and his own University of Glasgow did not found an economic chair as his memorial until the end of the nineteenth century. Of his principal successors, Ricardo was a stockbroker and John Stuart Mill a clerk to the East India Company. It was only with Jevons and Marshall that leadership in economic thinking passed, it may not be finally, to the Universities and that the Universities set full value on it. Marshall, may I say, was a greater economic historian than he let the world know. He had discarded as irrelevant to his main purposes more historical knowledge than many men acquire. There are some massive fragments of these *rejecta* in the Appendices to his volume on *Industry and Trade*, of 1919. He was eager to get historical work done. Long ago—I owe the personal reference to his memory—he pointed out to me tracts of economic history which needed someone's work. Then he pointed at me and said—"Thou art the man." I hesitated then, for Acton's power was on me, as I hope it still is. But Marshall has prevailed. To him, as well as to Cunningham, the foundation of this chair is a memorial. May it be enduring.

The term economic history is rather young; but the thing, the systematic inquiry into economic aspects of recent or remote history, is just about as old as most other systematic modern inquiry. Like important parts of economics, and so much in the physical sciences, it goes back to what Dr Whitehead has called the Century of Genius. Neglecting early anticipations and the casual economic asides of historians, Sir William Temple's *Observations upon the United Provinces* of 1672 and John Evelyn's *Navigation and Commerce, their original and progress* of 1674, though the latter is one of the slighter efforts of that distinguished Secretary of the Royal Society, might perhaps be said to mark the beginning[1].

[1] The books quoted here are of course only a selection of what seem to me the most important. For a far fuller survey, to which I am much indebted though I do not always agree with it, see Prof. Gras, "The Rise and Development of Economic History," *Ec. Hist. Rev.* vol. i. no. 1, 1927.

They really have a common problem—what are the historical causes of the economic strength and the economic weaknesses of Holland? What are the forces which, as Evelyn said, have "built and peopled goodly cities where nothing but rushes grew?" Forty years later, the same problem still occupied the mind of a very old and very distinguished Frenchman, who has sometimes been mentioned as a father of economic history, Pierre Daniel Huet, Bishop of Avranches, at one time sub-tutor of the Dauphin under Bossuet and—I am told—an elegant scholar. He had planned and directed the publication of the Delphin Classics. At the age of 86 (1716) he had published a small octavo *History of the Commerce of the Ancients*, written many years before to oblige Colbert, a book which as an English critic said is "chiefly a History of Sea Fights and Naval Expeditions" and, as a Scottish critic added, "pays no sort of regard either to chronology or cosmography." At the age of 87 Huet followed it up with a more substantial *Memoir on the Commerce of the Dutch*, written some ten years earlier, in the manner of Sir William Temple.

In the interval between these two attempts to help solve a problem in current politics by an appeal to recent economic history, the urgency of a very different problem had led a Cambridge man into a more fundamental and exact economico-historical inquiry. The matter can best be made clear by quoting the rather long title page of his book, which appeared anonymously in 1707. *Chronicon Preciosum: or, an Account of English Gold and Silver Money; the Price of Corn and other Commodities; and of Stipends, Salaries, Wages, Jointures, Portions, Day-labour etc. in England, for Six Hundred Years—shewing from the Decrease of the value of Money, and from the Increase of the value of corn and other commodities that a Fellow, who has an Estate in Land of Inheritance or a perpetual Pension of Five Pounds per Annum, may conscientiously keep his Fellowship...though the Statutes of his College (founded between the years 1440 and 1460) did then vacate his Fellowship on such condition.* The College is of course my own; the author who faced this great case of conscience was William Fleetwood, subsequently Bishop of Ely, a noted preacher who had given in a sermon delivered before the University in our chapel on Lady Day, 1689, a classic account of the life of a Fellow of King's: "We are here at perfect Ease and Liberty, free from all other cares and troubles than what we seek...entirely vacant to the pursuit of Wisdom, and the practice of Religion." It has been burned in on us these last ten years that nothing makes history, exalts and abases men and classes and kingdoms, like changes in the value of money. Lenin knew it. Those changes are perhaps most potent when their working is slowest and little noticed. Fleetwood first traced these slow movements over a long period. His method of studying them was unexceptionable, though he made mistakes of detail as Adam Smith pointed out. For prices he went to his College muniments because, as he wrote, "our General Histories do mostly give us the Prices of Things, which are extraordinary, either for Cheapness, or for Dearness; whereas the College Accounts deliver faithfully the ordinary and common Price of most Commodities and Provisions." He is the father of all the historians of price, who are the most exactly scientific of all historians; for, as Professor Eddington says, "what exact science looks for is not entities of some particular category but entities with a metrical aspect." Thorold Rogers in the nineteenth century followed Fleetwood into the muniment rooms in search of such entities. There is still abundant material there unworked.

Though Fleetwood's more learned contemporary, Thomas Madox, is not usually classed as an economic historian, for his interests were primarily legal, yet his *History of the Exchequer* (1711) claims mention because, with his later *Firma Burgi*, it laid the foundations of the exact study of medieval public finance; because it initiated a profitable alliance between economic history, in the narrow sense, and the history of institutions; above all, I think, because it stated in a couple of sentences all that ever need be stated, by an economic or any other kind of historian, about the duty of documentation. "For I think it is to be wished, that the Histories of a country so well furnished with Records and Manuscripts as ours is, should be grounded throughout...on proper vouchers." And again—"for my part I cannot look upon the History of England to be completely written, till it shall come to be written after that manner."

The next really important landmark, a critical landmark, was, I would suggest, Hume's Essay *Of the Populousness of Ancient Nations* (1742). He was concerned to prove that this populousness had been exaggerated. When it is remembered that he was arguing against the opinion "that there are not now on the face of the earth, the fiftieth part of mankind, which existed at the time of Julius Caesar," and that this opinion was Montesquieu's, it will be realized how strong was the myth of antiquity, how much sceptical discipline the best minds of Europe needed before they would consent to apply rational quantitative tests—or quantitative probabilities—to historical tradition.

The thirty years following the publication of Hume's *Essay* might be called the age of the annalists. In 1747 the Rev. John Smith, LL.B. (of Trinity Hall) published his *Chronicon Rusticum Commerciale*, or *Memoirs of Wool*, into which his notebooks vomited, but in good chronological order, extracts and analyses of every statute, proclamation, pamphlet and debate bearing even remotely on wool and the woollen industry with which years of diligence had filled them. In 1763 came the three heavy volumes of Adam Anderson's *Historical and Chronological Deduction of the Origins of Commerce*. Anderson was for forty years a clerk in the South Sea House and he had that unselective fondness for the accumulations of his leisure often found in men of affairs, and occasionally in scholars. When they would not go into his annals he pushed them into prefaces, surveys, excursuses, and appendices. He was the forerunner of a series of Scottish accumulators and dictionary makers—Sinclair, Macpherson, McCulloch, Macgregor—who in the next seventy or eighty years heaped up material, not always

well sifted but always useful, for the economist and the historian.

Meanwhile Scotland had given with Adam
Smith the man who used and stimulated the
accumulators, turned annals into rationalized
history and unassorted observations into
economic philosophy. He called his book a
"speculative work" and it was only in the
avowed digressions, and particularly in the
great digression in which he used and improved on Fleetwood's account of the changes
in the value of gold and silver, that he
adopted the pure narrative method, though
there is much of it in the chapters on colonies
and on the growth of towns; but his writing
was informed throughout with all the historical knowledge of his day. What is more,
there were always present to his mind the
interactions and contrasts of the economic
and the non-economic factors in national life.
Witness the famous section on the expense of
institutions for the education of youth, from
which comes the known quotation about the
greater part of the public professors at
Oxford having "for these many years, given

up altogether even the pretence of teaching," or the less known historical comment on musical education among the Greeks, which he thought had probably "no great effect in mending their morals." Smith's history was of course not like Madox's based on manuscript "vouchers": occasionally it may have been made to serve those general propositions which he wanted to establish: in detail it has sometimes been proved wrong, as was to be expected; but never before or since in the development of economic thought have historical and analytical workmanship been so finely blended as in the *Wealth of Nations*. I say "before" because one must not forget that nine years earlier yet another Scotsman, Sir James Steuart, had published a book which some German scholars have set up as a sort of rival to Smith's; a book whose very title, *An Inquiry into the Principles of Political Economy*, Smith might have taken for his own, had not he and Steuart—as Professor Cannan has pointed out—happened to have the same publisher; a book which like Smith's justifies its political title by the extent of its author's historical knowledge; yet a book which in spite of the German scholars, and in spite of the possibility that Smith sometimes conveyed from it without adequate acknowledgement, cannot stand beside the *Wealth of Nations*.

Within a few years of Smith's death (1790), and in the early troubled years of the French wars, there appeared Sir Frederick Eden's *State of the Poor: or an History of the Labouring Classes in England from the Conquest to the Present Period* (1797) and the first edition of Malthus' *Essay on Population* (1798). Eden's book is a remarkable piece of work—he was only thirty-one when he published it—perhaps most remarkable in the way that it anticipates the social inquiries into wages, dietaries, employment and standards of life which a modern economist connects with such names as Charles Booth and Seebohm Rowntree. But it is also, unless I am much mistaken, the first attempt to write some sort of an economic history of the common man. No doubt it is far too much a survey of laws about him, and he is regarded too much as potential pauper. The research, the first hand personal inquiry, is best in the contemporary sections. That is why the book is a mine for the historian of to-day. Yet the conception is there, the conception of an historical process determining the conditions of current problems and the material happiness of humble people.

Malthus' *Essay*, in its first form, was more dogmatic than historical. But in five succeeding editions he heaped about it historical material and what statistical material was available, almost burying and at certain points deflecting the original dogmatic framework; until it became something like a history of population and of the working of his positive checks upon it. He ransacked the classics, books of travel, general histories and such books—then very few—as the *Divine Order in the Vicissitudes of the Human Race* of Pastor Süssmilch (1707–1767), the man who has been called "the first statistician in the modern sense." One can imagine how Malthus would have welcomed some significant scraps of exact evidence from the ancient world recently collected for us by Mr W. W. Tarn—how 79 Greek families who received Milesian citizenship at the close of the third century B.C. contained 118 sons and 28 daughters; and how only 6 families out of 600 in second-century Delphic inscriptions reared two daughters. "No natural causes can account for these proportions," Mr Tarn writes. The positive check of female infanticide is the explanation, and for those times and places we can now measure its strength.

With Malthus' historical discussion of population, following on Hume's correction of legendary views, the men of the late seventeenth and eighteenth centuries completed a first, imperfect, reconnaissance of the field of economic history. They were mostly specialists. Only Adam Smith had got glimpses of the whole territory and a clear view over much of it. The professed scholars among them had begun rather apologetically. "The greatest (though I will not think the Best) part of readers," Fleetwood wrote, "will be rather apt to despise, than to commend the Pains that are taken in making

Collection of so mean things, as the Price of Wheat, and Oats, of Poultry, and such like Provisions." But he hoped "before he had done, to show you, that the Observation of these little things may be of good Use in the Consideration of great Affairs," and he consoled himself by thinking that "if any ancient Greek or Latin Writer had taken the Like [Pains] and left such a Collection you would have had the Salmasius's, the Graevius's and the Gronovii almost out of their wits for very joy." (To-day one who can rely on those ample English records of which Madox spoke, and the printed records which have succeeded them, is sorry for the Gronovii because no ancient Greek or Latin writer did.) But when the nineteenth century trampled in out of the storm the timidest pedant had no longer need to apologize. The prices of the mean things, leaping up, showed their power in great Affairs. The common man in France had lighted a candle of rich men's houses. Peasants were being emancipated in Prussia, to show that a King could do for his people as much as the Revolution.

Open-fields and commons were being cleared away in England as a safeguard against hunger; for the old fear that there might not be men enough for the wars was being replaced by the new fear that there might be too many mouths to fill. A commercial empire, just ceasing to be able to feed itself, at grips with an agrarian empire—which also went hungry in years of bad harvest—was learning the truth of that old saying about the Dutch ships: "except they go the people starve." Modern chemistry was just beginning to show its industrial power; and in 1800 Messrs Boulton and Watt completed their 312th patent steam engine.

Watching all this, a beggared French nobleman of irregular life, who at sixteen had fought for American Independence and who died in 1825, decided that the only thing in the world that mattered was industry in the widest sense of the word. (He allowed, for example, that artists and professors were industrial persons of an inferior kind.) Politics and religion, liberty and equality, were toys. Sane history was the story of the freeing of industrial forces. The only form of parliament worth having was a parliament of economic experts, as we should say, occupied with schemes for industrial progress. He founded a school and the school a sect—the St Simonians. The claim of economic history to dominate all history had been formulated, but vaguely and unphilosophically, by a man mainly interested in the future. To make a philosophy of it, the so-called historical materialism, was Karl Marx's work. Writing in 1894, eleven years after Marx died, Frederick Engels claimed that the Master in 1845 had made the "discovery, that everywhere and always political conditions and events find their explanation in the corresponding economic conditions." Marx wrote no treatise on historical method. Those who have collated and examined his various pronouncements most carefully are of opinion that he only meant that the ultimate causes of all great social changes are to be sought in the economic conditions of the age under review. Engels, as we see, claimed for him more than that; but then Engels was a pious disciple.

Even Engels did not argue that each particular historical happening, of whatever kind it may appear to be, is economically determined. Fanatical Marxists—with some people who would be surprised if they were so described—seem now and then to have held this doctrine and the chase for the economic clue is conspicuous in much of the historical writing of the last thirty or forty years. There is, of course, even an economic explanation of Calvary, which those who remember the rich man and Lazarus and the tables of the money-changers must at least weigh. Fantastic though some economico-historical adventures may be, I suppose that all historians are now so far in agreement with Marx as to be unable to think of major political upheavals and important social changes into which economic causation does not enter, however great their distrust of purely economic explanations, of those who overlook so-called historical accidents, and of that kind of single-cause history which will pack the fall of Rome into an epigram.

For myself I am not convinced that the

search for the economic clue has even yet gone far enough. (Should anyone say that I am professionally bound so to think, I admit that there is such a risk.) I expect, for example, that when the English economic history of the seventeenth century has been fully worked out—there is a great deal yet to do—we shall find, not an explanation of Bunyan's spiritual distress in a lag in the rise of tinkers' wages, or of Milton's harder traits in his parentage—Milton the elder was a scrivener, though a musical scrivener; and we are just learning that the seventeenth-century scriveners were often money-lenders and incipient bankers—not these, but all kinds of new things about the causes of political unrest, the successes and failures of political parties, and that profound change in the social atmosphere of England which occurred somewhere between Shakespeare and Defoe. We understand that change much better already since Mr R. H. Tawney wrote two years ago his *Religion and the Rise of Capitalism*. But has our general history taken properly into account the fact—fairly well established

long ago, though in need of more inquiry—
that the food-purchasing power of wages
was lower in 1600–1650 than it had been for
three hundred years or has been since?

Marxism, by attraction and repulsion, has
perhaps done more to make men think about
economic history and inquire into it than any
other teaching—especially in Germany, Italy
and Russia. But not until Marx's main book,
or rather that part of it which appeared in his
lifetime, had circulated for over fifteen years
in Germany and had been translated into
French and last of all into English—that is
to say not until the late 'eighties of the nineteenth century—did the stimulus of Marxism
become so effective that economic history
began to fall naturally into the Marxian
categories. Its most remarkable product has
been the *Moderne Kapitalismus* of Werner
Sombart, which first appeared in two volumes
in 1902 and reached the sixth volume of a
remade edition in 1928. It is a gigantic
attempt, full of learning, eloquence, strong
feeling and strong words, to review and ex-
plain the whole history of European capi-

talism since the Dark Ages. Sombart is not a Marxian—far from it—but he is a passionate admirer of Marx the historian, the man who, as he says, "discovered the new world" of capitalism, who posed all the historical problems of its origin and the speculative problems of its end. Neither precisely historian nor precisely economist (he isolates too much for the first and narrates too much for the second) Sombart is assailable from both camps. But I feel towards him much as he feels towards Marx. No one should handle any part of the industrial or commercial history of the last thousand years without weighing what Sombart has said of it. He may easily disagree. He is certain to be stirred and informed.

Strong as the Marxian influence has become —it is very conspicuous in that great book of two years ago, Rostovtzeff's *Social and Economic History of the Roman Empire*—it was by no means the first influence making for a revival of economico-historical studies in the nineteenth century. Marx himself might have argued that the economic conditions of the first half of the century imposed these studies on humanity. It may be so—in the realm of ultimate cause. But the immediate causes, working strongly in the decade before Marx made his "discovery," were German nationalism; English pride in England's recent economic achievement; and the ambition of a young German professor to master economic fact and thought historically as his elder contemporary, Savigny, had mastered jurisprudence. I have in mind List's *National System of Political Economy* (1841–4); Porter's *Progress of the Nation* (1836–43); and Roscher's *Political Economy according to the Historical Method* (1843).

List was not a professed historian: he was a propagandist and politician of genius. But his main contentions led the economist straight into history. They were that economic policies (in this case Free Trade) are not of universal application; and that economists must not confine themselves to studies of wealth and problems of exchange conceived of as all on one plane; but must think of living changing nations on different and shifting planes, and of the growth of their productive powers. Porter, a dry and rather limited statistician, did not look much beyond his own century but laid the foundations for the quantitative treatment of modern economic history, with the aid of material for the collection and issue of which by the Board of Trade he was himself largely responsible. Roscher, a man of more learning than discernment, contributed very little to the body of economic thought, though he put it in its historical place; but in a long life (he died in 1894) he saw the growth of a great German school of economic historians and historical economists to whom the historians of every other nation are heavily in debt. Fifty-nine years ago, for example, Brentano started the modern study of English medieval gilds. In a volume published last year the wonderful old man complains that his views have fallen into undeserved neglect latterly. His name is only one among many German names in English economic historiography, Ochenkowski, Schanz, Held, Hasbach. There is still no book in English on English railway history and policy to compare with one written by a Göttingen professor, Cohn, in the nineteenth century; and the last general survey of the medieval economic history of England written in German—it appeared by a gloomy accident in 1918—can hold its own with the last general survey written in English.

As economists, that is to say as explainers of the economic life of an existing bundle of communities with a view to its ultimate betterment—I hope the definition will be accepted—as economists, I believe that the German historical school have gone bankrupt. The aim of their left wing at least was to dissolve economics in history. Their last great leader, Gustav Schmoller, to whom Cambridge offered an honorary degree in 1913 and who died during the war, after many years of pure historical work of the first order, tried in a two-volumed *Principles* in 1900–2 to illustrate this doctrine that "historical delineation can become economic theory." "He solves nothing," I find that I noted on the flyleaf at the time, having started his book with high hopes and acquired much information of all kinds from it. My view seems to be accepted in his own country. He did not succeed "in erecting a new scientific structure" in the place of the existing body of economic doctrine, a German historical critic wrote last year, adding—"that this situation was not satisfactory seemed clear to everyone." Sombart, who is full of contempt for the mere historian on the one hand and for the more refined economic thinkers on the other, has accomplished more because he has used more abstraction and made all his learning bear on one problem—though a vast and complex one—but his principal accomplishment is historical. He has not as yet taught us very much about the contemporary functioning of capitalism, though he claims to have uttered the "modest last word about it"; and his very gratifying praise of some of our recent Cambridge economic manuals and other lighter English theoretical work suggests that he might have appreciated our severer analytical thought, given the patience to master it.

Here in Cambridge, I think I may say, economist and economic historian are at peace. We know our limitations. We can sit happily side by side under Adam Smith's great umbrella labelled *An Inquiry into the Nature and Causes of the Wealth of Nations*. The Professor of Political Economy will not cry out because I do not read a mathematical article (which, for the rest, I might not understand) dealing with taxation "in a purely competitive system with no foreign trade," though, for all I know, it may throw much light on the Nature of Wealth and its taxability. I shall not resent his indifference to what I take to be the final demonstration, just completed by archaeologists and air-photographers, that the now familiar strips of the medieval open-field were unknown in Roman or Celtic Britain; although the change to the strips—being connected with an improved plough—was no doubt in its time a Cause of a Nation's Wealth.

The economic historian knows that economists who wish to give precision to their study, and to fill its emptier categories with fact, are thoroughly dissatisfied even with the mass of statistical material now existing, and are always working for more. He knows, for instance, that any close causal handling of the problem of unemployment cannot go behind the first publication of the Trade Union figures in the 'eighties; and that fairly adequate material for the exact study of trade cycles is just now being assembled for the first time. So he understands the relative indifference of the more exact economists towards what little he can say about unemployment during the Napoleonic Wars or about what look like beginnings of a trade cycle under the Tudors. He knows, no one better, that any quantitative treatment of remote social phenomena to which he can aspire—even the simplest: how much of England was enclosed in 1700? how big was an average gild? how heavy was the burden of the Danegeld?—that any such treatment is likely to yield results on a plane of truth lower than that attainable, if not always attained, by the economist. If by good fortune the economic historian has one set of measured facts for a remote date—certain truths so far as they go—he will often lack that second set which leads to the illuminating conclusion. He may know the amount of wool exported in 1273 but not its price schedule, the amount of the Danegeld but not the taxable capacity of England. Very conscious of this, he is most unlikely either to rush out from under the ordained umbrella or to claim the whole shadow of it for himself. This is all on the assumption that he knows about modern economics and its opportunities. I have come across historical writers who seemed not to know these things well.

If the economic historian has his modesties in presence of the pure economist he also has his pride. He is proud because, by definition as historian, he is one to whom the tangled variety of human life is attractive in itself; one who will study alterations in the tangle for the love of it, even when his information is such that he can never hope to pick out with assurance the forces at work, or measure exactly the changes brought about by the aggregate of them between dates x and y. He cares for the beginnings of things as such. He likes to trace the growth of institutions which have been moulded by man's need to keep alive and man's desire for comfort and prosperity—village communities, trading companies, Christmas goose clubs—although he may not be able to number the community, read the balance sheet of the company, or find the slate of the goose club. It pleases him to know that in such and such an age caravans took the golden road to Samarkand, and that in such another age they went no more, even if he cannot count the camels or prove—what he always suspects—that the total amount of the rose-candy spikenard and mastic conveyed was really trifling. Some men—George Unwin was one—have turned to economic history mainly because it is so full of workings together for useful ends, of community life of all sorts, not because it is particularly rich—as of course it is—in "entities with a metrical aspect." Others may like best what is odd, individual, idiosyncratic in the story of how men have kept alive and as comfortable as may be. It is, in fact, a story full of attractive oddities. They weary of the general averages of statistical truth and of such human sequences as may be plotted in graphs. Others again may care most for the unmeasurable thoughts which make the measured things. But these all are within the covenant, very well within it. The historian likes his companions to be as varied as his matter; and happily there is no excluding definition which says that to be economic an "entity" must be "metrical."

Yet; yet; it is the obvious business of an economic historian to be a measurer above other historians. For this the worker among English records—manuscript or printed— has immense opportunity, as Madox said and as the many Germans, Americans, and others who have worked among them, to our very great advantage, well know. While grateful to all, one is glad to think that the history of English prices begun by Fleetwood and carried on by Adam Smith was resumed, in the 'sixties of the nineteenth century, by Thorold Rogers at Oxford without outside inspiration. I think I am right in saying also

that the similar work of continental scholars
—as for example, that of the Vicomte
d'Avenel in France—was planned in definite
imitation of Rogers. It was natural that such
work should start here, because no continental country has anything approaching in
continuity and completeness the records of
Merton on which Rogers began, or the other
College records to which he turned; just as
none has a national record so old and so
complete as our Domesday, from which my
King's colleague, William Corbett—after
half a lifetime of work—was able to give us,
just before he died, a picture of William of
Normandy doling out the loot of English
land almost as exact as might be the secret
report of some syndicate distributing the
profits after a successful *coup* on the rubber
market. It is only a comparatively few years
since the Record Office first made available
the series of Customs Accounts and Port
Books, from which it is possible—given
enough labour—to work out much of the
English overseas trade from the later Middle
Ages in astonishing detail, though strict

measurement is not in this case always quite easy.

I tried just now to place the economic historian in relation to the economist. There is still a little more to be said about their joint relation to the historian without prefix. Forty years ago, and less, Seeley used to picture political economy as an invader occupying historical territory. "When each new human science has carved out a province [from history] for itself," he wrote in a very familiar page of his *Lectures on Political Science*, "will not the residuum at last entirely disappear?" Historians, we recall how he went on to argue, must fall back on the province which no one can take from them— that of the State, its growth, its forms, its functions, the Kingdom of Political Science. If I thought in terms of war and the carving out of provinces, I believe I could draft operation orders for an economist's raid on that kingdom also, leaving the Professor of Political Science to draft his orders for the defensive battle; but that is not how I think.

When I picture the place of economics in

history modestly, I sometimes see the economic worker as a sort of osteologist, a collector and student of historical bones, old defective fossil sets and pretty complete sets of well-articulated modern ones. I think of him saying deferentially to the pure historian, who in his fancy is sometimes himself—it is for you to call on Clio. "Come from the four winds, O breath, and breathe upon these... that they may live." I have given you to the best of my power—he falls back into specialist's jargon—the osseous structure of successive types of societies and nations, the stiff working parts, the things which condition their activity and determine its forms. Now set them to their fighting and law-making, their songs and their prayers. I am no rival. Yours is the higher work. I want to help.

It is easy, when modesty wanes, for us economic historians to glorify this bone business of ours. We can hint at the very unreal or lop-sided or dropsical historical monsters which might be reconstructed—have indeed been reconstructed—through neglect of it. Or we may choose some quite different comparison which gives more honour to the economic worker. But whether we are modest or proud, and whatever the comparison, we shall admit that there are things in history beyond and, in the scale of values, above his things. We shall not, I think, accept Seeley's easy solution that the historian can "afford to be sketchy and summary" on "economical questions" because a specialist has taken them from him. His practice was better than his doctrine; for in his *Life and Times of Stein* he gave a full account of peasant emancipation in Prussia.

Insisting on the full observance of his practice, even denouncing those who do not follow it, we shall still recognize economic history for what it is, a help-study—pardon the Teutonism: I know no English equivalent —a link-study between history and economics; and we shall make it our business, like the common men of our narratives, to work together with all willing historians, as with all willing economists, for useful ends.

www.ingramcontent.com/pod-product-compliance
Ingram Content Group UK Ltd.
Pitfield, Milton Keynes, MK11 3LW, UK
UKHW042141280225
455719UK00001B/18

9 781107 674264